Allan Potts.

Natural North

Allan Potts FRPS

View from Tosson Hill, Rothbury, Northumberland

Photographs and text:Allan Potts

Design:Nick Ridley

First published in 2000 by Zymurgy Publishing, Newcastle upon Tyne, United Kingdom.

Printed by Midas Printing (HK) Ltd

Zymurgy

ISBN 1-903506-00-X

Foreword

The North of England is rich in natural beauty, both in its landscape and its wildlife, in contrast to the industrial image which has coloured the perceptions of recent generations. From the Pennine fells, through forests, fields and old pit heaps, to the rugged coast lashed by wind and rain, flora and fauna in some cases abound, in others survive precariously. There is a message of hope, with the return of otters to our hills, and other wildlife to abandoned industrial areas, and a message of caution, that we must be more responsible with the wildlife in our care. This book conveys, with stunning photography, the wealth of natural history that is such an important part of our northern heritage, and there can be few people better qualified to produce it, than Allan Potts.

Allan's farming experience in the shadow of industrial Tyneside, his extraordinary photographic talent, his knowledge of nature, and ability to interest and educate the reader, ensure that this book will find a ready place in my book case, and I am sure, many others.

The Duke of Northumberland

Contents

I am particularly indebted to Eric Bird and George Wall (and the goodwill of their wives) who have assisted me in many ways in the field, sharing information and knowledge.

A special mention must go to naturalists: Duncan Preston, Steve Taylor and John Wilson.

For their commercial services: Ken MacMillan, management and staff at Colorworld Laboratories, North Shields.

Staff and management at H.A. West, Team Valley Trading Estate, Gateshead.

My photographic agent, Bruce Coleman.

The Northumberland Wildlife Trust and Whitley Bay Photographic Society.

For design, layout, scanning and editing through hundreds of slides: Nick Ridley. Without his many hours, patience and commitment this book would not have been possible.

For assistance to the publisher: Dolly Potter, Gill Ferrell and Cindy Winter.

I am grateful to numerous other individuals and organisations who have provided a wide range of support over many years.

I would like to dedicate this book to my wife, Mary for her great help and understanding.

Also my daughters Helen, Jane and son Andrew for their constant support.

Allan Potts FRPS

The distinctive male red grouse.

View of Stuart Shield Meadows, Stanhope Common, County Durham

The Lonely Fells

The north's open moorland is desolate and peaceful. Usually the soil is poor and acid, supporting only heather, ling and tussocky mat-grass. The fells may have been shaped by man, but are still some of the last wild places in England. For wildlife, these windswept hills are an ecological niche. Many birds, mammals, insects and flowers are totally dependent on this moorland habitat.

It is fascinating to visualise how the area now known as the Pennine and Cheviot Hills might have appeared after the ice age and, perhaps more dificult, to imagine how the wildlife evolved in these harsh conditions. Today, this area has been colonised by many animal species that have made it their home. It is an uncompromising world of prey and predator where the dashing merlin and fearless peregrine are the hunters of the northern hills.

To the visitor, the sounds of birds across the lonely fells is inspirational. Birds such as curlew, red grouse, golden plover and ring ouzel, are all noted for their distinctive calls.

Female red grouse

The species that has pride of place across the moors is the red grouse. This handsome bird, favoured by the shooting fraternity, is related to its Scandinavian cousin the willow grouse.

The well-managed moors of the north support a healthy number of red grouse which can be seen throughout the year. They are the most distinctive game birds across the lonely fells, exploding into the sky when flushed, flapping their wings and descending steeply to the ground, barking out their distinctive call, "go-back, go-back".

The cock proclaims his courtship ritual by jumping into the air with wings outstretched, then diving abruptly to the ground fanning his tail and stretching his neck, challenging all other rivals.

For most of the year food for the red grouse is plentiful, but during the cold winter months the supply can drop dramatically. As a permanent resident across the fells, it is the only one untroubled by extreme weather conditions. If times are hard it will burrow below the snow for food; low-growing plants like heather and bilberry will be dug out and readily consumed.

Because of these extreme conditions, they have evolved with thick downy feathers, helping to prevent heat loss. Even their feathered feet act like snow shoes. Only this extreme hardiness keeps them alive during difficult times.

One of Northumberland's most famous rivers is the Coquet, wild and beautiful, regarded by many as one of the most scenic rivers in the country.

From its source in the marshy grounds at Coquethead, it runs through the remote farming areas of Upper Coquetdale, before reaching the North Sea at Amble, a journey of 55 miles from its head water.

Along the fast flowing upper reaches are numerous falls, giving the water plenty of oxygen to support rich aquatic life. The most common insect species are stonefly and mayfly, creating a food source for many forms of wildlife that feed from its turbulent waters.

The high rainfall in the hill country creates some of the best fishing rivers, including the River Tweed, which is considered to be the finest in the North of England.

The wild valley of Upper Coquetdale

The river Coquet carves its way through the bedrock, on its journey to the sea

In full spate, the River Coquet carries a peat stain from the open moors

Where there is rushing water you will usually find the dipper. It is a plump, wren-like bird with a distinctive snowy white breast. It can often be seen curtsying, quivering its wings, and blinking its protective nictitating membrane. Its sweet warbling song can be heard above the river sounds, so characteristic of the upland waters.

These wonderful characters are quite unique in the way they hunt for food. Perched on a rock they dive into fast-flowing water, and literally walk on the river bed in search of crustaceans, a behaviour pattern common to all dippers.

In early spring they are the first birds to commence breeding. Their nest is always near fast-flowing water, usually under a low bridge or the overhang of a river bank and, on occasions, hidden behind a waterfall.

The Dipper, much-loved character of the Northumbrian rivers

The curlew has a long lifespan of approximately thirty years

Characterstic to the moors is the curlew, one of the first wading birds that returns to the fells each spring. Wintering around coastal areas of the British Isles, it feeds on small crabs, shrimps and lugworms. However during the breeding season, its diet changes to worms, frogs, insects and their larvae.

The curlew is easily distinguished from other species, by its long downward curved bill, used to probe for hidden invertebrates.

A clutch of four curlew eggs

Thirl Moor, Makendon, Upper Coquetdale, Northumberland

Newly hatched curlew chick appears from the brood pouch

Golden plover

Dotterel

Dotterel spend the winter in Northern Africa. Greenshank winter over a much larger area including the coastal areas of the southern British Isles, Europe and North Africa. In the spring they are merely passing through the northern hills on their way to their breeding grounds in the Scottish Highlands, and beyond to sub-Arctic and Arctic regions.

A ring ouzel nest in a juniper bush

One predator that has declined in numbers is the merlin. Once every moor had this bird of prey. Today they are increasing again in a few places. Hunting mainly meadow pipits and sometimes insects, they are very selective feeders, taking the most nutritious food for their diet.

Flying fast and low over the heather, they hunt the ground for their prey. The adult male, known as a tiercel has blue-grey upper parts. It is a fearless little predator that is very agile when hunting, following every twist and turn of its quarry's flight.

Nesting among the heather, the merlin lays three to five eggs, cream in colour with heavy red-brown freckles. Incubation lasts around thirty days and the young will leave the nest after approximately twenty-six days.

During the middle ages they were used in falconry by women. Ladies found the merlin light and easy to handle and they took pride of place during a sporting day.

Merlin chick at 25 days old

The kids never venture far from the safety of the herd

The River Breamish at Bleakhope, North Northumberland:- typical feral goat country

Northumberland is home to the historic wild goats of the Cheviots. They are the descendants of domestic goats and have been wild for well over two hundred years.

No hill or gully is too difficult for these agile, sure-footed animals. Throughout the summer, they tend to remain high up on the fell tops, browsing among grass, heather and bracken. They are extremely hardy; only during the most severe weather conditions are they forced to move down to the valley bottoms.

The curled horns of the ram grow continually and are never shed. Over their life time, the horns can reach 76cm in length. During the rutting season in mid-October, they will fight for supremacy so that only the strongest and fittest animal will pass on its genes to the next generation.

The females give birth to their kids in January

The dominant ram

Looking from Simonside towards Thropton in Northumberland. Areas of old heather have been burnt,
allowing many plant species to regenerate.

In early summer, the northern countryside is one of lush green meadows and rolling hills. While the
fell sandstone creates the shape of the landscape, the vegetation determines its appearance.

Throughout the year the pattern of the hills shows a subtle range of colour, with heather and
grasses mixed with patches of bilberry, bracken, and sheep sorrel carpeting the ground.

The flora may not be the most outstanding in the country, but it is nevertheless a diverse and
wonderful blend of arctic and continental species that have colonised despite the fluctuations of the
weather.

Over many years, due to climatic change, plant species have changed. Some flowers have colonised
new ground or moved on from areas which are no longer suitable for them to survive.

In the marshy areas, communities of cotton grass and swords of sphagnum moss grow. This varied
habitat is also the home to a delicately balanced community of plants, many with extraordinarily
beautiful flowers.

The flowers that are readily seen are foxglove, pansy and thyme, along with the other common
varieties.

Wild pansy

Thyme

Foxglove

The snipe among sheep sorrel

River Coquet running down to Linbriggs in Upper Coquetdale, Northumberland

The female oystercatcher returning to its nest and eggs

The rolling hills of the Cheviots and their fast-flowing rivers epitomise the region's scenery. On occasions the landscape is stark and beautiful.

The dominating quality of this almost treeless countryside is the amount of space and the lack of disturbance.

The density of wildlife is usually low when compared with the arable farmland and woodlands of the more sheltered lowland regions, but this remoteness is invaluable for many animals.

The markings of the oystercatcher stand out amongst other birds. It was once confined to shingle shores and river beds but it now breeds in the northern hills and is moving into the farmland nesting areas.

The redshank (right) with its elegant long red legs, is another wader of the uplands. This bird is extremely alert at all times. If intruders approach it will rise into the sky, crying out a hysterical volley of harsh piping calls.

The redshank - sentinel of the lonely fells

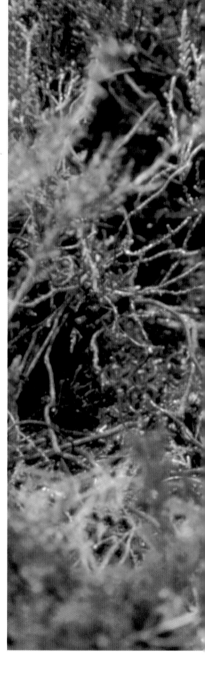

Owls depend on sharp, wide-ranging vision for spotting prey in the deep undergrowth

These birds need to be successful when hunting, especially with hungry mouths to feed

Of all the birds of prey, none can compare with the short-eared owl. Their catlike eyes and quizzical appearance have great appeal.

Once they were regular breeders throughout the moors and fells, but today they are a rare sight. The ears, which give the bird its name, are just small tufts of feathers, having no purpose other than decoration.

Like all owls, they have very sensitive hearing and extremely keen eyesight enabling them to pinpoint the faintest rustle in the grass. However, they differ from other owl species by being diurnal, that is to say they hunt during the hours of daylight. Quartering over the moorland in search of small mammals, they are silent in flight. Taking their prey by surprise is their means of attack.

The short-eared owl lays its eggs at two-day intervals, and commences incubation as soon as the first egg is laid. Each egg will hatch after around twenty-six days so there will always be an age difference between the eldest and the youngest. When the food supply is poor the larger chick will eat the smaller: one of the laws of nature where only the fittest will survive.

Short-eared owl with 3-week old chicks

Bank vole - the owl's main diet

Life is a nightmare for the bank vole. Hunted by foxes, badgers, stoats and weasels, and under airborne attack from kestrel, hawk and owl, it must always be on the look-out for its enemies.

Voles breed constantly throughout the year, as long as the weather is kind and there is plenty of food available. Having a life span of around eighteen months, a vole will produce young of its own within a few weeks of birth, so there is always a constant supply of these small animals entering the food chain.

The Cheviots were formed some 380 million years ago when a number of large volcanic eruptions spewed out ash and lava covering some 350 square miles.

Much later, magma was pushed up from below the surface and cooled to form granite, creating the great sweep of hills comprising the Cheviot massif. Much of the area was then covered by a shallow sea which left a bed of sand around the foothills of the Cheviots.

A few million years on during the Ice Age, glaciers gouged out the contours, shaping hills and valleys like Barrow Scar, as we know them now.

Today this landscape is looked upon as an area of untamed beauty, with wide horizons and lonely farm settlements. It is understandable that in the 1950s it was declared a National Park, covering some 1,030 square kilometres

The raven

Barrow Scar, the remnants of the glacial period

Although the National Park is not really a wilderness, it still offers some of the most strenuous walks along the old drove roads and ridge paths that once harboured the infamous Border Reivers; gangs of thieves and rustlers who terrorised the hill land.

This wild terrain has long been the home for many species of wildlife. One of the most spectacular birds of prey is the peregrine. Flying high in the sky over moorland and valleys, it pursues its prey at a tremendous speed.

Along with the peregrine is the raven, another bird of the hill country. Ravens are the scavengers of the fells, their deep, black colouring giving them a sinister appearance, which probably accounts for their reputation as the heralds of ill omen. Constantly on the lookout for an easy meal, they can often be seen tumbling in the thermal currents, crying out their unmistakable deep throaty call.

The peregrine falcon

Palmate newt

The head water of Three Stone Burn (above) lies at the foot of Hedgehope Hill in Northumberland. At 714 metres above sea level, it is second only in height to Cheviot in the Cheviot hills. This wetland area is invaluable for creatures that make this their home. Amphibians, invertebrates, insects and reptiles survive here throughout the year. Unspoiled and managed solely by nature, this area needs to remain an unaltered ecological corner for its indigenous wildlife. These boggy areas are acidic, with extremely low nutrient levels. Home to a wide variety of insect species, specialised flora have developed other ways to supplement their diet, such as the insect-eating sundew.

Adder

Common frog

Plants like the round-leaved sundew need to acquire extra protein if they are to survive in these poorer soil conditions. They excrete a sticky liquid over their leaves which traps small insects such as the common blue damselfly.

Four-spotted chaser

Emperor moth

Cauldron Snout

Cow Green Reservoir

Heather

Just below the source of the River Tees lies Cow Green Reservoir, constructed in 1970 to supply water to Darlington and Teesside. High up in the Upper Teesdale National Nature Reserve, the average summer temperature is similar to that of Iceland.

The Tees continues to flow though the falls at Cauldron Snout, High Force and Teesdale.

To survive the short summers and harsh winters in this area, plants have evolved and adapted. Growing in exposed situations they developed a dwarf, cushion-like habit, with dense hairy leaves that protect them from wind burn and freezing conditions.

The sugar limestone escarpment at Teesdale is made up of crumbling rock which has been constantly eroded by frost, wind and rain, but has retained much of its dazzlingly rich flora from just after the glacial period.

Plants like Teesdale gentian, birds-eye primrose and globe flower are some of the treasures from the past that are in danger of being lost forever due to the effects of global warming.

Wild pansy

Birds eye primrose

Globe flower

Teesdale spring gentian

What is intriguing about wildlife is the variety of so many different creatures, an almost inexhaustible chain of related and unrelated animals whose existence has evolved over millions of years.

Unfortunately some species have come to the edge of extinction, while others fight to make a comeback.

The otter, a most appealing animal, is a born survivor. Rivers like the Coquet and the Tees have begun to see the return of these creatures.

To them, freshwater streams are home. Overhanging banks provide secluded areas to build their holts and the water is a source for food, particularly eels and brown trout.

The male red grouse in breeding plumage - Stanhope, County Durham

It is almost impossible to see the female grouse when she is incubating her eggs as her mottled colouring blends in so well with the vegetation.

A female red grouse peers out from the seclusion of the heather

Male black grouse

Incubating grey hen (black grouse)

Another game bird of the northern hills is the black grouse. Unlike its cousin the red grouse, it is declining in numbers. It is hoped that a solution may be found, before black grouse disappear from moorland areas altogether.

One of the best areas for black grouse is among the rolling fell land of Middleton in Teesdale. The remoteness of the area provides a haven for this elegant bird

The black cock's display with rival males is one of strong aggression, with full-blooded fights that take place on the lecking ground.

The female black grouse, known as the grey hen, has an incubation period of 27 days. Her nest is always well hidden among the heather or bracken with a clutch of around eight eggs that are usually laid into a deep, well lined nest.

When the chicks hatch, they will leave the nest almost immediately, growing their flight feathers within three to four days and they are able to fly within a month.

A newly hatched black grouse chick

The red grouse normally produces a clutch of eight eggs

Middlehope Moor, Upper Weardale in County Durham

Dog & Stick Country

Through the passage of time, man has created a patchwork of small and irregularly-shaped fields. The landscape changed around five thousand years ago, when early farmers began to clear wooded areas. Generations have used 'dog and stick' to bring the hills into pastoral use.

As agriculture has changed the natural environment, so wildlife has adapted. A number of bird species like the; barn owl, pied wagtail, starling, swallow, and even the kestrel regularly exploit used and disused farm buildings.

Lapwing

It is now unusual to see horses plodding across open farmland. John Dodd and daughter Frances and son-in-law David Wise, use Clydesdale horses on their farm in Hexhamshire, Northumberland. Although it takes longer than mechanical methods, they feel that their method is in sympathy with the countryside.

Mixed farming was essential. Turnips were mainly grown for livestock feed, sown in the spring, it was an important time of year

Ploughing with Clydesdale horses. These "Gentle Giants" were used in farming until the mid twentieth century

Harrowing corn in after drilling covers the seed and protects it from
birds, enabling it to germinate and produce a more even crop

Camera-shy Clydesdale, Robin, was not easy to photograph. He galloped off when approached.

The rolling landscape of Hexhamshire

Bottle feeding an orphan lamb

Shepherding would be an almost impossible task without the collie. A good working collie is very agile and extremely intelligent. It has the ability to work instinctively among sheep, able to gather and split on command. It can respond to a shepherd's whistle over a mile away.

Shearing

Swaledale sheep at the Wall's farm in Upper Weardale

Hill farming methods have changed little over the centuries. The weather has always created problems and always will.

Shepherds do not have an easy life, working long hours on the fells. During lambing in the spring they are 'on call' at all times. Sheep shearing in June and July is followed by gathering and dipping in late summer.

On the more exposed hills the blackface and smaller Cheviot are kept. Swaledale sheep are the most popular breed in County Durham; a dense undercoat helps them survive the harsh weather conditions. The larger border Leicester is popular at lower altitudes, valued as a meat producing animal.

Quad and dogs, invaluable for gathering sheep

Swallows are prolific, they live in both lowland and upland countryside. Centuries ago swallows commonly nested in coastal caves. Farm buildings are now the usual place to find swallows and it is unusual to find them nesting in caves.

Each year they will travel from South Africa, where they spend the winter months, a much warmer climate than the north of England. Their navigational system allows them to return to the same nest site as where they bred the previous year.

Hungry young swallows have a voracious appetite, they will consume many thousands of insects caught by their parents.

Shillmoor, Upper Coquetdale

Barn swallows

A lonely disused cattle shed at Snowhope in the Durham dales becomes the nursery for a family of kestrels

Constant encroachment on the countryside has resulted in the loss of habitat for wild-life. Some species have welcomed the arrival of man and set up home in buildings.

The kestrel hunts on grass verges, along motorways, main roads and on the moors of northern hills. It has recently become an urban bird, nesting in holes and ledges on churches, blocks of flats and factories

Its shrill call is a "kee-kee-kee" which is used during the mating display or as a distress call.

The kestrel's agility on the wing is impressive. Hovering with its tail fanned, its head remains motionless, even in strong winds. This enables the kestrel to pin-point prey, before diving to the ground to make an instant kill.

At ten days old the chicks are constantly looking for food. Their diet consists mainly of mice, voles and small birds, occasionally frogs, insects and earthworms

The kestrel's eyesight is extremely keen, so important when hunting

Four eggs, white with heavy brown markings laid in a shallow nest

At three weeks old these chicks will soon be ready to leave the nest

A red-legged partridge

A common grey partridge chick leaves the nest within hours
of hatching

The red-legged partridge was introduced from France around fifty years ago; it is bigger, plumper and more brightly coloured than the common grey partridge.

Between ten and twenty eggs are laid and it is known for two or more birds to lay in the same nest, clutches of up to forty eggs may be found.

After hatching, the chicks are extremely vulnerable during the first two weeks .Wet weather and predators lead to the greatest loss of life.

The pheasant was first recorded in England in 1059 but it is believed that the Romans introduced them from Asia. The cock-pheasant is by far the largest and most brightly coloured game bird. During cold winter months they take advantage of the free food that is available around sheep troughs

Freak storms in early spring at higher altitudes force species like the curlew to nest lower down, away from the cold of the high fell tops.

Breeding amongst grazing animals presents problems. It is interesting to observe the adult curlews defending their territory against intruders. While sitting on the nest they will open their wings and strike out with their bills. This curlew has allowed the grass to be grazed right up to the edge of her nest, without the sheep trampling her eggs.

View at Carter Bar looking towards the Northumberland and Scotland border

The snipe's long bill allows it to probe deeply into marshy ground for invertebrates

One remarkable feature of the snipe is its colouring. The streaked brown plumage provides her with excellent camouflage on the nest

The remote, wild open spaces found on Northumberland fells provide a good breeding environment for many birds, including the snipe. To breed successfully birds need to defend the territory around their nests, the size the territory is dependent on the food requirement. Predatory birds with a specialised diet forage over a large area, whilst the lapwing finds a food supply at its feet.

When rival birds meet on overlapping territories, they will put on an impressive display, often showing off plumage and making threatening noises.

The snipe marks out its breeding area by flying steeply into the sky. Descending, it splays out two outer tail feathers that vibrate, producing a quivering, drumming sound.

The female snipe incubates the eggs for about twenty one days

The mistle thrush has a great liking for berries of the parasitic mistletoe and it feeds heartily on the hawthorn during the autumn. Without the vocal talent of the song thrush, its distinctive rasping call is usually a deterrent to drive away intruders.

The countryside has changed considerably over the last century. Changes brought about by farming are least noticeable in livestock areas.

Permanent meadows favour wildlife. Tussocky grass is important for insects and provides a place for hibernation during winter months.

With livestock production, dung encourages a great number of insects which break down droppings, returning nutrients to the soil.

In mid-April, the flush of new grass turns many pasture fields into an emerald green carpet. However, for ground-nesting birds this attractive landscape provides very little. There is no tussocky grass in which to conceal nests and little in the way of insects to feed on.

Fortunately, today more trees are planted by the farmer in an attempt to replace the natural habitat for hedgerow nesting birds, previously lost when fields were merged.

A typical livestock farming scene at Knowesgate, north of Belsay in Northumberland

The open cup-shaped nest of the chaffinch

The male chaffinch

For all birds, nest building is an instinctive behaviour. Some species will build on rock faces, some will select old farm buildings, others nest on the ground or even in a burrow, while others build in hedgerows and trees.

The chaffinch (above) produced an unusual, beautiful and complex nest design. The normal method is to use leaves that are woven into the nest with animal hair, but not on this occasion. This pair were very much more selective, using mosses and lichen stripped from the branches of the host tree, the common alder.

Unfortunately, the result was not a success. As the eight chicks grew larger, the nest became overcrowded. Four of them where pushed out and fell into the river below. Two days later, the remaining chicks died when cold torrential rain swamped their home and the adults deserted.

A grasshopper emerges into the world. Within a few hours the wings dry out and it will begin making a rasping sound by rubbing its hind legs together.

At the outer edges of meadow fields where grass is long and ungrazed it is possible to find many insects. Grasshoppers and crickets make buzzing and churring sounds.

Almost any area of heather or meadow field with a good mix of herbaceous plants will attract insects. The insect's role is to pollinate plants such as the birdsfoot trefoil, knapweed and foxglove and long-spurred flowers such as orchids.

The red admiral butterfly is one of the most beautiful species to be seen feeding on nectar

Elephant hawk moth caterpillar

The rosebay willowherb is often called fireweed because it is an early coloniser of areas that have been burnt. Its downy seeds are released into the wind and are blown far and wide across the countryside.

The elephant hawk moth is a vivid pink. It feeds during late evening on the rosebay willowherb. The name is derived from the appearance of the caterpillar, whose body resembles an elephant's trunk. It deters predators by extending its thorax, which is marked with eye spots.

An amazing eye of this amazing moth

The brightly-coloured elephant hawk moth

Nookton Fell near Blanchland on the border between County Durham and Northumberland

Roe deer kid

The shapes and patterns of the northern landscape are almost completely man-made. Drystone walls enclose heather moors and green meadows.

In areas close to woodland it is possible to find roe deer. These animals avoid contact with humans, most active at dawn and dusk they are usually seen singly or in family groups.

Roe deer buck

A field of oilseed rape

Sowing spring beans

Arable Heartland

Arable land is farmed intensively. Modern agricultural techniques and their effect on the environment are controversial. Almost every job is now mechanised; the machinery makes use of computer technology and satellite communication. As farm equipment has developed the number of farm workers has declined, fields have increased in size and hedgerows have disappeared.

Arable farming takes place on premium quality land. The soil tends to be light and loamy, free from underground bedrock and is well drained. The climate is also more hospitable than on high land, enabling farmers to cultivate a greater variety of crops.

Crop production is driven by the demands of domestic and international markets. Arable is the most profitable farming sector, bringing in high revenues and bumper yields. The most valuable land for man is the poorest land for wildlife.

Hawthorn hedgerows, however, provide a haven for wild-life. They grow rapidly, producing a wonderful habitat for nesting birds. In the eighteenth and nineteenth centuries, hawthorn was planted to create field and farm boundaries. If left to grow wild, it can reach a height of well over ten metres.

Harvesting wheat

The early 1970s was the era of the 'barley boom' when widespread barley production changed the face of arable countryside. It was grown almost continuously without a 'break crop'.

A large proportion is now exported to Europe and the Middle East through the Port of Tyne.

Wheat is also a profitable cereal crop; modern varieties produce a high yield.

Flour from hard wheat is used for bread making; biscuits and pastry use soft wheat. The lower quality wheat is compounded for animal feed.

Wheat is sprayed with herbicides and fungicides to maximise the yield

Combined harvester

Regina barley

Mallaca, a high protein wheat for bread making

Scentless mayweed

Everyone is attracted by wild flowers, they bring a mass of colour to the countryside. Many species thrive despite the use of herbicide due to their prodigious rate of reproduction. Thousands of seeds ripen and fall to the ground; a proportion every year will germinate. Fortunately many wild flower species are protected by law.

Germander speedwell

Field poppies

Male lapwing

Newly hatched lapwing chicks

Grey partridge

Seen in arable land are three species that symbolise the open countryside: the brown hare, partridge and lapwing. The lapwing is often identified by it's "pee-weet" call. The grey partridge is noted for it's explosive leap into the air, followed by a repetitive "krikrikkrik..." call.

Brown hares, unlike rabbits, live permanently above ground, giving birth to the leverets in early spring.

Arable farmland at Clennel, Northumberland

Six-day old leverets

The barn owl is a most striking bird. Unfortunately its ghostly figure flying in the evening is not as common as it used to be. When hunting, it relies mainly on its acute sense of hearing to pinpoint the sound made by its prey.

Farmers have always valued its ability to control rodents and occasionally owl lofts were incorporated into farm buildings.

On average, a clutch of five young will consume two rodents a night. They stay in the nest for up to twelve weeks, in which time they eat their way through around four hundred voles, mice, rats and shrews.

A parent barn owl returns to the loft with a field mouse to feed the chicks

Male blackbird

Song thrush

Common garden snails

Few species have exactly the same diet as their neighbour, so reducing direct competition for food.

The thrush family eat mainly earthworms and other invertebrates. Hunting during daylight hours, their perception does not need to be as acute as that of nocturnal birds. Song thrushes break open snails on stones, blackbirds sit back on their haunches, pulling out earthworms from the ground.

Through evolution bird species have developed different types of bill. The greenfinch have stout bills enabling them to crack open seeds, wild fruit and berries. Like many other finches, they have become regular garden visitors.

Greenfinch

Hawthorne hedgerow at Backworth, Tyne & Wear

A fox cub

The polecat has been re-introduced into northern countryside

The survival of predators is important in maintaining the balance of nature, even in highly man-managed arable areas.

Foxes are opportunists, rabbits and rodents are their favoured food. They also eat earthworms, insects, other invertebrates, carrion, blackberries and the fruits of hedgerows.

Other predators include stoats, weasels and polecats.

A meal for many predators - the field mouse

Stoats and weasels feed on rabbits. Numbers have increased recently due to the growth in the rabbit population

Black-headed gulls

L ate summer is a busy time for arable farmers;
as soon as crops are harvested the land is then
ploughed. Many black-headed gulls home in on
the bounty of worms that come to the surface.
Over eighty per cent of black-headed gulls nest
inland, selecting boggy areas around lakes and
gravel quarries.

Autumn ploughing

Woodhorn Colliery Museum, Ashington

Grey heron

A subsidance pond at Backworth

Industrial Heritage

Ever since the industrial revolution, heavy industry has dominated much of the urban landscape of the north of England. As mines opened, villages and towns were built to house the communities dedicated to the extraction of coal and the world's first railways were built to transport the coal. Mining is now extinct in most of County Durham and Northumberland, and is a fraction of its former scale in Yorkshire.

The collapse of many mine workings has created a number of new ponds and wetlands. Nature has been assisted by the work of conservation groups. The Northumberland Wildlife Trust has established a nature reserve on the site of the old Rising Sun Colliery. The Wallsend Swallow Pond, a shallow lowland wet area, is a good example of what can be achieved. A number of other wetlands have been successfully created including; Holywell Pond near Whitley Bay, Cresswell Pond near Druridge Bay and numerous small sites across the region.

A wide range of birds now live around the ponds and wetlands formed from old mine workings. Swans, ducks and geese along with the heron and kingfisher now depend on these new habitats. The busiest time of year is the autumn, when flocks of mallard, widgeon and teal are joined by visitors such as greylag, pink-footed and Canada geese. In winter months the ponds are a haven for waterfowl. Whooper swan, tufted duck and resident species the mute swan, coot and moorhen can all be seen.

Nesting little grebe

Birds that nest close to water are vulnerable to changes in the water level. When water levels rise gradually, breeding birds will add material to keep the nest and eggs out of danger. In the case of a flash flood, grebes have been known to lose their nest and eggs. The little grebe, sometimes referred to as the dabchick is an expert swimmer and diver. It is the smallest of the grebe family, feeding on sticklebacks and a host of water insects. It can be found on inland waters throughout the north of England.

The great crested grebe is larger than the little grebe, noted for its elaborate and facinating courtship display. It was once threatened with extinction because its feathers were used to decorate ladies' hats; now protected, its numbers have increased.

Naturalist, Eric Bird attempts to rescue a little grebe nest after torrential rainfall

Great crested grebe

Great crested grebe

A curious cow inspects great crested grebe eggs

Female great crested grebe returns to eggs

Rosebay willowherb

The decline of mining and heavy industry has provided space for wildlife to reclaim land from man. Disused railway lines and embankments provide undisturbed habitat for many wild flowers such as toadflax, trefoil, vetch, rosebay willowherb and, in a few special areas, early marsh and spotted orchids. These plants in turn provide a habitat for insects and invertebrates.

On a summer's day, moths and butterflies bring the countryside alive with a variety of colour. Clumps of nettles and the purple flowers of knapweed and thistle attract species such as the red admiral, small tortoiseshell, peacock and common blue butterflies. Thousands of other insects and invertebrates thrive on wild flowers and in turn many wild flowers need the insects for pollination.

Caterpillar

Common blue butterflies mating

Peacock butterfly

Soldier beetle feeding on scentless mayweed

Marsh helleborines grow in damp areas

Orchids are wild flowers of great beauty with varied shape, colour and design. Bee orchids have developed a method of pollination by stimulating the sexual desires of the bee. The lower furry lip of the flower looks strikingly like that of the abdomen of a female bee, attracting the males to mate so pollinating the orchid!

Broad leaved and spotted orchids growing on reclaimed land

Rare bee orchids growing in the grounds of the Philips electronics factory, County Durham

Mallard duck

The mallard makes use of its own down in nest construction

The mallard nests away from water and occasionally in urban gardens. They take their broods to water after hatching.

The garden is a sought-after habitat for many wildlife species, providing ponds to drink from and flowering herbaceous borders with insects to feed on.

Urban gardens provide food for wildlife

Robins nesting in a horse's hay net.

Robin.

Nature produces some genetic rarities like this albino frog. A true Albino has a pink eye and is marked by congenital absence of pigments in the skin, which is usually white. However on this occasion the frog has turned a peachy colour, due to staining from stagnant water.

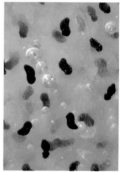

A single frog can lay an enormous number of eggs in early spring, and yet in many areas they struggle to maintain their population. Pollution, disturbance by man and predation by water fowl accounts for the loss of significant numbers.

Common frog

The decline of natural habitats has created the need for wildlife to adapt and fit in with the changing environment. It is difficult at times to understand why animals are attracted to a strange habitat, when there are more suitable areas at hand. Perhaps the most unusual example was the moorhen that built its nest out of a newspaper on the boundaries of a landfill site at Seghill in Northumberland

Moorhen

Moorhen's nest and eggs

Quarries can also provide a home for birds; in particular the sand martin and oystercatcher can be found breeding in quarries. On one occasion, a pair of little ringed plover selected the stony breeding environment of a disused quarry in County Durham.

Oyster catcher returning to nest and eggs

Little ringed plover with newly hatched chick

Sand martin nesting in a gravel quarry

Nesting kittiwakes, Quayside, Newcastle upon Tyne

As more land is lost to city development, so wildlife has adjusted to this pressure. Green fields have given way to acres of concrete in towns and cities. Whilst city life is inhospitable and sterile for most wildlife, tall buildings are being used by cliff-nesting birds, whose natural habitat could be many miles away. A classic example is the kittiwake traditionaly found on sea cliffs, now using high-rise buildings for breeding ledges.

At one time, starlings were as common as weeds in a neglected garden, but even this bird has shown a marked decline among our cities and parkland. Brash, aggressive and ruthless, it is an opportunistic bird, but a devoted parent.

Towns and cities may offer more shelter than some parts of the countryside. Foraging among litter bins, rooks will feed off discarded take-away meals and waste.

Starling

A pair of rooks built this nest close to Eldon Square shopping centre in the centre of Newcastle upon Tyne

Common hazel

Sycamore

Sycamore

Ash

Secretive Woodland

Ever since the first primitive saplings turned their heads to the sun, trees have been the mainstay of a diverse forest ecosystem.

Trees live much longer than any other forms of life and their green canopy provides a habitat for countless birds and animals. Even when a tree dies life does not end; dead branches become a home for bacteria, insects and other parasites. As it decomposes over many years, all of its remains are returned to enrich the earth of the forest floor.

Thousands of years ago, forests covered much of the north of England. The oak played an important part in pagan religion and in Norman times wolves and wild boar roomed the great forests. Huge oaks, such as the one in Hulne Park, the Duke of Northumberland's estate, could be well over four hundred years old.

The woodland environment is a joy to see during the day. Through the night, fungi push their way to the surface.

Beech trees at Bolam, Northumberland

First introduced from the Balkans in the late eighteenth century, the horse chestnut grows vigorously with large beautiful leaves, producing elegant wax-candle-like flowers.

The well loved horse chestnut is easily identified by children, who have enjoyed playing conkers for generations.

Mature horse chestnut

Horse chestnut leaves

Beech catkins

Bluebell wood at Harbottle, Northumberland

Wild garlic in Blagdon Dene, Northumberland

The uniform stands of ramson wild garlic, creates a snowy white carpet . Its prolific growth takes over the forest floor excluding other plant life.

Primrose and woodland violet

Hedgehog forage in woodland glades

Primroses are attracted to open forest glades. They flower early, before trees come into leaf. They are frequently accompanied by wood anemone and woodland violet. Violets produce seed much later in the season, when weather conditions favour germination.

A slow-worm wakes from hibernation. It is in fact a legless lizard which feeds on slugs and insects.

Juvenile barn owl familly

Although the barn owl's name might not suggest it lives in trees, it may have been a true woodland species, long before man ever established his first primitive building.

The barn owl is not as demanding as other owl species. When selecting a nesting site, however, they do not like modern farm buildings, preferring hollow trees.

The little owl is one of our smallest owl species. It hunts during the day, favouring early evening around dusk and has a diet made up mainly of insects, earthworms, voles, mice and birds to the size of starlings. Now a rare sight in the country landscape, it can sometimes be seen sitting out on telegraph wires or dead branches.

Adult little owl

Juvenile little owl peers out of tree hole nest

Female tawny owl

The constant chattering of birds in a Weardale woodland, led me to these chicks sitting out on a branch of a black alder. The distress call is a sure sign of a predator. The intruder may often be a tawny owl. It commences egg laying in early February, and sometimes the fledged chicks may be seen in late March, near their nesting hole.

Tawny owl chicks

Incubating woodcock

Woodcock nest and eggs

The woodcock sitting on the nest is well disguised, the camouflage of its feathers blending with the surrounding vegetation.

It prefers damp areas to raise its young, as there is always a ready supply of invertebrates hidden in the woodland floor. The long bill enables it to probe deeply in soft earth for worms, insects and their larvae.

Newly hatched woodcock chicks

Nettlehope Hill, Northumberland

Juvenile buzzard

As it flies over coniferous woodland, the buzzard can be mistaken for a golden eagle. Soaring on a thermal, they scan the countryside for rabbits, although the birds that I photographed also brought in a regular supply of frogs to feed the chicks.

Buzzard familly

Bullfinch

Long-tailed tit

Compared with deciduous woodlands, conifer plantations are not the ideal habitat for wildlife. The trees support fewer insects, there is very little undergrowth, and the pine needles on the forest floor smother any vegetation that tries to emerge. There are very few holes and little dead bark for nest sites, but the gloomy corridors of conifer trees do provide a limited range of specialist breeding habitats.

The characteristic conifer forest birds are the siskin, coal tit, goldcrest, and crossbill. Around the forest edge long-tailed tit, great tit, blue tit, chaffinch, bullfinch, blackbird, song thrush and robin are among the species most frequently found. The most specialised feeder of them all is the crossbill. It has an unusual large scissor-like curved mandible, used to prize open ripe cones to pick out the seeds.

Male crossbill

Male and female crossbills

Kingfisher with bull-head fish

Kingfisher with minnow

The shy and elusive kingfisher is one of Britain's most brightly coloured birds. Its flight is low, straight and swift with rapid wing-beats

Woodland streams and rivers are habitat for breeding kingfishers. During winter if streams freeze over and food becomes scarce, they move down to estuaries and coastal rock pools. Kingfishers feed on small fish, molluscs, frog spawn and aquatic insects. Unusually, for the bird world, small fish are killed by beating against a stone or branch before consumption.

When feeding the young, the parents always present the fish to the chick head first. This prevents the gills and fins from sticking in the chick's throat.

Woodland stream

The adult goldfinch feeds its young

Flycatcher chicks

In the natural world animals do not live in harmony. Predation is vicious and necessary for the survival of predatory species. The jay eats young nestling birds. On this occasion goldfinch chicks were snatched from the nest, possibly to feed the jay's own family. Flycatcher chicks also feature on the jay's menu.

The adult goldfinch left to collect food and over a period of twenty minutes the jay took all five chicks

Jay

Typical home for the green woodpecker, an old beech tree

The green woodpecker does not depend on the garden environment for food, being a true woodland species throughout the year. They are much larger than the great spotted, with an unmistakable yaffle type call. Preferring broad leaved woodlands, they will chisel out their breeding chamber in hardwood trees.

Green woodpecker famlly

Male great spotted woodpecker

The great spotted woodpecker is widespread throughout many of the northern coniferous and deciduous woodlands.

In the spring it makes a distinctive drumming sound to mark out its territory.

Many woodland birds nest in holes previously excavated by woodpeckers.

The great spotted is an adaptable species, with a varied diet, it rarely has difficulty in finding food, mainly larvae and insects. Similar to the jay, it will snatch young nestlings to feed to its own young. During the winter, it leaves woodland areas for easy pickings from garden bird tables and basket feeders.

Silver birch woodland

Juvenile (lower) with female great spotted woodpecker

Of all the varied habitats for badgers, woodlands are undoubtedly the finest. There is an abundance of food; berries, nuts and worms, as well as dense cover for breeding, sleeping and feeding.

Quite often they will make their homes on the outskirts of a wood. Their setts are extensive systems of underground tunnels and chambers, often excavated and occupied by many generations of families. There are several entrances, some out in the open, and others concealed by thick undergrowth

Woodland rabbit

Juvenile red squirrel

Red squirrel in winter

The red squirrel is undoubtedly our most popular small native mammal. The strongest concentration can be found in northern woodlands. Its body is perfectly adapted for climbing trees with speed and agility made possible by light bones and powerful long rear legs.

Red squirrels do not hibernate for they cannot survive for more than a few days without food. Pine cones are the most important single item in their diet. Hanging by their limbs, they can feed upside down with the greatest of ease. When food is plentiful, they will store it by digging small holes in the ground, covering them with soil and leaf litter.

The red squirrel is fortunate in not having the pine marten on its doorstep, although there is some evidence that a few are present in Northumberland. They feed on squirrels, birds and other small mammals such as voles.

Their climbing agility and speed is remarkable; running up a tree trunk with their sharp claws, they will easily out manoeuvre any squirrel.

The grey squirrel, introduced from North America during the early part of the twentieth century, is now spreading rapidly northwards, much to the detriment of the red squirrel. The grey is simply too successful when competing for food. Being a much larger and more aggressive species, it is able to take over the red's woodland environment.

Both species have predators such as pine martens, foxes, birds of prey and (near the urban fringe), cats and dogs. Squirrels in turn are predators, feeding on insects, eggs, and young birds. Most of their food is detected by smell; woodland fruit buried months ago is located in this way, enabling them to survive the lean winter months.

Pine marten

Grey squirrel in summer

Fly agaric

Hedgehog

Bracket Fungi

Crested coral fungi

Common stinkhorn

Mushrooms and toadstools are the stuff of folklore and legend. In mediaeval times they were considered to be the 'poisonous ferment of the earth'.

Although people in the past could generally identify the edible and poisonous types, many of us are now a little wary of fungi. A reliable field guide is a wise precaution.

Hedgehogs are great scavengers and are mostly active at night. They will readily consume beetles, caterpillars and earthworms. Hibernating during the winter months in a sheltered nest of leaves and grasses, they rely on the body fat built up in the autumn.

Fairies bonnets

Puffballs

Aspen

Beech

Autumn is marked by lowering temperatures and shortening daylight hours. It is also the time of the year when trees produce a larder of food in the form of wild berries. Animals respond to the shorter days and lower temperatures by eating more food, to build up their body fat before the onset of winter.

Birch

Red squirrel

The northern countryside in winter, especially after a fall of snow, is surely one of the great spectacles of nature.

For some wildlife, climate change and milder weather makes life a little easier during the short days of winter. However it can create problems for creatures which hibernate, as it may encourage them to emerge early. Hedgehogs are particularly at risk if they end hibernation too soon.

Mistle thrush

Blackbird

Gorfen Letch, Northumberland

North Atlantic grey seal

The Great Whin Sill, Northumberland

Tidal Rhythm

The coastline provides a breeding habitat for shore birds and mammals. Man's recreational use of the coastline has led to an enormous loss of breeding areas over the past forty years. Areas of the most significant value are protected by the National Trust and English Nature, whose duty is to promote the conservation of flora and fauna on the fragile dunes.

The natural world is full of contrasts. While our shore birds live alongside man, further out to sea, the Farne Islands are a fortified sanctuary. Here great colonies of sea birds crowd the high cliffs, continuing an intricate cycle of life that has lasted for many thousands of years. The constant clamour of nesting sea birds and the nitrogen-rich smells of these 'wildlife cities' are unforgettable.

Puffin

Every year breeding birds that have spent the summer months on the vast areas of the Arctic tundra flock south to the north of England. During the winter the Arctic is inhospitable, and yet in the short Arctic summer it offers almost unlimited living space, a profusion of insect life and almost twenty-four hours of daylight each day in which to hunt and feed their families.

The most northerly visitor to our coastal region is possibly the knot, sometimes referred to as the 'Canutes from the far north'. They breed in northern Siberia and northern Greenland, in bare stony tundra that becomes locked with snow and ice during the long winter months.

The North Sea provides a regular supply of food washed in by the tide. This ebb and flow of nature's rhythm punctuates life for shore birds that feed from rock pools and sandy beaches.

Another migrant that seeks out winter refuge on the coast is the elegant grey plover. It breeds in the high arctic tundras of Russia and Siberia, at this time of year it is a sombre grey colour. Come the spring, it moults its winter plumage, when the entire face, breast and belly, turn into striking black and grey.

All birds have individual character. For me, the sanderling, another Arctic visitor, is by far the most interesting. Chasing the tide like miniature clockwork toys, they scamper up and down the beach always just in front of the breaking waves, jumping in the air at the last moment, as though it is imperative not to get their feet wet!

With frantic bursts of energy, flocks of sanderling, knot and purple sandpiper, are constantly on the move. Rising into the sky when disturbed, they chatter out a chorus of calls before settling once again, snatching a few morsels of food from the rock pools and mud flats, before the crash of the next wave.

Knot at St Mary's lighthouse, Whitley Bay.

Sanderling

Grey plover

Knot

Marsden Rock before the collapse of the arch

A flight of kittiwakes at Marsden Bay

Marsden Rock after the collapse of the arch. The pinnacle (right) had to be demolished in the interests of public safety.

Northumberland's dramatic coastline has been sculptured by the sea and weather. The shoreline is the constantly evolving product of this erosion as the rock succumbs to the daily pounding. A recent example is the collapsing of the limestone roof at Marsden Rock, South Shields.

While the sea is the great destroyer of the natural world, it is also home for hundreds of marine species.

Marsden Rock has always accommodated sea birds; the most striking is the kittiwake. Hugging the smallest of ledges, their nests appear as though they will tumble into the sea at any moment. Some years nature can be cruel and whole colonies are blown or washed from the rock face, by extreme weather conditions.

Kittiwakes are not opportunistic feeders like herring gulls, who enjoy food from a wide number of different sources. Kittiwakes are carnivorous, feeding directly from the sea, they are dependent on a variety of fish and small invertebrates.

Soft limestone rock that has seen many years of constant erosion

Also found on Marsden Rock are cormorants, voracious feeders and strong underwater swimmers, among the many sea birds who live by diving for food. They are the only ones that do not produce waterproofing oil. They can often be seen standing on a rock with wings outstretched, drying out their feathers.

Cormorant

Breeding kittiwakes

The shoreline at Marsden, South Shields

Fisherman inspecting a catch of lobsters

Fishing boats come in all shapes and sizes. Open boats that catch crabs and lobsters work from beaches or natural harbours. Larger expensive trawlers work away for a longer periods of time, storing their catch on ice, or in chilled seawater tanks. In biological terms modern sophisticated trawlers are voracious predators, with an uncontrollable appetite.

Prawns, a great delicacy

Lobsters, a declining species

Sunderland fishing boats at the mouth of the Wear

Holy Island

Turnstone

Herring gulls

Fishing harbours were built to enable the catch to be landed in deep water without risk of the vessel grounding. They also provide a safe haven from the angry seas. This haven is also a refuge for wildlife. The eider duck often makes use of this shelter during bad weather.

Rafts of eider duck are a common sight along the north eastern coast. Breeding on the Farne Islands and nearby Coquet Island, this part of the east coast is their most southerly breeding range.

Of all the sea ducks the eider is the best known and most numerous. Nicknamed the cuddy duck after St. Cuthbert, who lived a sparse existence on this windswept rock twenty metres above sea level. It is said to have been his favourite among all the bird species of the Farne Islands.

The eider is very much at home on the sea, bobbing about, riding the strongest sea surge and calling out its crooning 'ah-oo, ah-oo'.

Amble harbour

Eider duck

Eider drake in boat reflections

Dunstanburgh Castle

After the weather, the main problem facing wildlife that nest among the seashore and sand dunes, is the tramp of human feet. For waders like the ringed plover, oystercatcher, arctic and little terns, the ideal nesting place is a sand or shingle bank, out of the way of the incoming tide. Unfortunately these areas are also popular recreational spots.

One of Northumberland's rarest breeding birds is the little tern. The little tern faces its own particular dangers. As it nests so close to the high water line, its nest may be washed away and its eggs floated off by an exceptionally high tide. Help is however on hand for these birds that nest in a precarious position. National Trust wardens monitor the nests during the breeding season and move those at risk onto old fish boxes that have been filled with sand. The boxes are gradually moved up the beach, away from the incoming tide. This relocation causes no disturbance and is readily accepted by the little terns.

Common lizard sunning itself

Ringed plover in coastal dunes

Little tern

For the little tern a disused fish box makes a safer environment

Seahouses harbour, the gateway to the Farne Islands

Arctic tern

Bridled and common guillemot

Shag

Razorbill

The renowned Farne Islands, a group of some twenty-eight islands situated off the Bamburgh coast, house a bird sanctuary, loved by naturalists. The islands are owned by the National Trust.

The Farnes were used by St. Aidan and St. Cuthbert, as places to meditate in solitude.

In early spring, thousands of oceanic birds arrive at these high sea cliffs for one purpose only, to breed. They have ridden the waves at sea for most of the year and it is only now that their reproductive cycle urges them back to land.

The sea bird life is quite exceptional, with teeming colonies of guillemot, razorbill, puffin, shag, cormorant, tern and kittiwake, along with gull and duck. These islands are busy sanctuaries until the end of the breeding season.

The south-west stack at Inner Farnes

Sandwich tern

Guillemot

Breeding birds on Staple Island

Nesting material is taken daily to breeding burrows

Of all the birds that fly the north eastern seaboard, my favourite by far is the puffin. This wonderful character is handsome, sociable and demonstrates stacks of personality with an amusing growling call, "har-har-harrr," as it woos its partner.

The most noticeable feature about the puffin is its large, brightly-coloured bill, used as a digging tool and as an advertising medium to attract a mate. When the breeding season is finished it sheds its bill, which is replaced with a less distinguished, short dark bill. Nesting below ground in burrows, they are safe from marauding gulls that are constantly on the lookout for unguarded chicks.

Once the puffin chick has hatched it will remain in the burrow for about forty days; then the parents will desert the fat nestling and it will be forced to leave the burrow to search for food. This usually takes place under the cover of darkness when few predators are about. Scurrying to the sea and leaving land for two to three years, it will not breed until it is four or five years old.

Birds enjoy socialising in the mid-day sun

It is amazing how many sand eels a puffin can hold in its bill!

The puffin uses its webbed feet as air-brakes

All creatures have their own individual charm; my favourite marine mammal is the seal, a sensitive creature with large intelligent eyes. Marine mammals are both sea creature and land animal. Seals return to land to mate, give birth and then return to sea.

The Atlantic grey seal that breeds around the coastal seaboard of Britain is found in great numbers on the Farne Islands and at Donna Nook in Lincolnshire. Breeding begins in October, when the bulls fight to establish their territory. While the skirmishes may look terrifying and involve a fair amount of aggression, more often than not only superficial wounds are inflicted. However the most dominant bulls can be heavily scarred around the head and shoulders as a result of battles.

Dominant bulls ward off rival males

A pregnant female rejects the sub-adult's amorous foreplay

The female grey seal on occasion, has the appearance of a sorrowful dog

Female Atlantic grey seal

Wildlife Encounters

Farming on the urban fringe has kept me in touch with the natural world at my back door. The countryside is very much part of my life and I have always had the desire to photograph nature. It is wild, beautiful, full of pattern and constantly changing. Photography is a unique medium for recording the natural world. It captures the complexity of the animal world and the environment.

Photography enables me to express myself creatively. It is possible to reveal beauty, capture significant events and record behaviour which many people never get to see. Successful wildlife photography needs to be visually exciting and informative.

To be a competent photographer, it is important to enjoy the outdoor world. Experiencing a wild fell in changing conditions, is every bit as inspiring as seeing animals in their natural habitat. Finding the locations and subjects to photograph can take days, weeks, months and sometimes even years. Wildlife photography in many ways is compulsive.

Frustration is very much part and parcel of encounters with wildlife. I remember once waiting five hours for that perfect lighting effect to enhance what was otherwise a mundane landscape. Sure enough, the clouds eventually broke and the sky cleared revealing glorious evening sunlight. An aircraft appeared from behind a storm cloud and flew directly across the area of blue sky, that was key to the composition of the photograph. Needless to say, the plume of white vapour trail destroyed the whole effect of that perfect image of a wild escarpment.

Moments such as these are typical. On another occasion the subject was a breeding pair of great spotted woodpeckers. Their nesting chamber was in a sycamore tree five and a half metres from the ground. So as not to create a disturbance, I spent two weeks gradually erecting a pylon hide. It was important to construct the hide over a period of days, so that the adult birds would not become anxious. If they became upset in any way, they are known to desert their young. As there was no way of estimating the age of the chicks, I was never quite sure exactly when they would fledge. Before I had the opportunity to expose a single frame, one by one, all the chicks vacated their nesting chamber.

The techniques for photographing animals can be simple or complex. The ability to compose an eye-catching photograph is not easy, and luck can be as important as good management. It is all about being in the right place at the right time, with the right camera and lens combination. When working in the field an understanding of the behaviour of the subject makes a power of difference. I have found it rewarding to concentrate on a particular species over a period of time.

The more sensitive a creature is, the more difficult it is to photograph. I have gained great satisfaction from my time spent photographing barn owls. Today they are an endangered species, a highly protected Schedule One bird. As a consequence of their

Ten metre scaffolding hide for photographing buzzards

Photographic Equipment Used by Allan Potts

35mm Single Lens Reflex Cameras

A modern single lens reflex camera has a host of technical features that make it the most practical camera for wildlife photography. The opportunity to use a range of different lenses makes it flexible. I use a Nikon but there are plenty of other manufacturers of SLR's to choose from.The cost of thirty-five mm film and processing is relatively cheap, making it is the best all round format.

Camera bodies used:-
Nikon F5, two Nikon F90X

Medium Format

Medium format has advantages, not as light and portable as a SLR. For land-scape photography my favourites are the 35mm wide angle and 105-210mm zoom.

Medium format used:-Mamiya 645 with 3 Sekor lenses; 35mm, 80 mm macro, 105-210 mm zoom

Panoramic

Extremely useful as demonstrated by the Panascape images within the book.

Panoramic Equipment Used:-
Hasalblad XPAN with 45mm and 90mm lenses.

Lenses

My most useful lens is a 500mm f4 autofocus Nikon, it requires the use of a tripod, it is invaluable particularly when photographing birds.

Lenses used:- 20 - 35mm zoom, 35 - 70mm zoom, 70 - 180mm Micro Nikkor Zoom, 80 - 200mm Zoom, 500mm Tel-ephoto.All lenses are auto focus.

Film
Mainly Fuji Velvia 50 ASA and Elite 100 ASA, occasionally Kodak Ekterchrome.

Tripod
A tripod is invaluable and will make a major difference to the quality of nat-ural history photography. It will hold the camera still, enabling the photog-rapher to concentrate on composition and focusing.

Tripods Used:- Bembo and Gitzo tri-pods plus the use of a bean bag.

Flash Guns
3 Nikon SB25
Quantum radio controlled slave unit

Bags
Lowepro camera bags

alarming decline they are protected by law and can only be photographed at the nest with a licence granted by English Nature.

My first encounter with barn owls was many years ago, before the great decline of the species in the north east. Owls have always been my first love, intelligent aristocrats of the bird world. A more symbolic description is "Lords of the Night". They are the most demanding species to photograph, requiring time and patience. They present many problems to the photographer, not least because they are nocturnal.

The owl loft where I took my first photographs was believed to be specially designed for the species, built in the early nineteenth century in the apex of a roof. There was no problem erecting a pylon hide inside the barn. The greatest difficulty was seeing the birds in total darkness! To overcome this problem, in January,

before the breeding season, I positioned a sixty watt lamp connected to a dimmer unit and a time switch. The time switch enabled me to control when the light would come on. After setting up the lighting equipment, it was left in place so that when the barn owls reappeared they would accept it as part of the building.

On return in mid May, I was pleased to find the female was incubating six eggs. Everything had gone to plan. Next step was to arrange the light to come on at nine-thirty in the evening, to coincide with the male feeding the female in the loft. It would switch off at three-thirty in the morning. The lamp, controlled by the dimmer, was set at a very low level of illumination, to avoid causing distress.

I spent the first evening observing their behaviour and was quite satisfied it was not causing any disturbance. Over the next two weeks, the level of brightness was gradually increased to a level that enabled me to focus and compose the subject. After allowing a further five nights to pass I decided it was now time to start the photography.

After arranging the electronic flash and camera equipment in the morning, I returned in the evening at eight-thirty, climbed up into the hide and peered through the viewfinder. I could make out the murky outline of the female in the darkness, as she crouched over her nest.

At nine-thirty the light came on as prearranged. For the first time I could see the beautiful creamy-white buff colouring, flecked with blue grey markings. As she gently moved upwards, four tiny pink faces appeared from under her downy feathers, so frail they looked quite unreal. As quickly as the chicks appeared, they disappeared under the warmth of their mother's body. Fluffing out her feathers, she settled down and continued to brood.

Looking out through the entrance to the owl loft, I waited for the male to arrive with food. The sun was beginning to set, there was a reddish pink glow in the sky. The tranquillity of the still evening air, was only broken by the evening call of a blackbird, as darkness approached.

Looking through my camera lens at a quarter to eleven, I peered straight into the eyes of the male barn owl, unaware that it had just flown in from the darkness of the night. Clutching a field vole in his talons, he called out with a long screech to the female. She stood up, revealing the four chicks that had been hatched at two-day intervals.

Obliging tawny owl chicks

Badger hide

eggs, she slowly tuck
into her brood pouch
settled down to incubate
them. I quickly exposed
fifteen frames. Monitoring
behaviour I noticed she
appeared to move her head
from left to right for no
apparent reason. Without
warning, the hide was hit by
a tremendous rush of wind,
followed by a deafening noise.
I have never been so close to
the after burners of a Tornado
jet fighter. Even the heat from
the engines was noticeable as
it banked while practising a
low level sortie.

The fright caused me to
forget momentarily about the
curlew. To my amazement,
the bird was sitting quite unconcerned, as though
nothing had happened. I later found out that it was
an almost daily air force exercise and the curlew was
now accustomed to their routine. Not only will I never
forget the incident, I shall always wonder how wildlife
adapts to the intrusion of man.

In order to photograph a group of badgers I set up
a hide close to a badger sett. At the site I sprinkled
honey-coated peanuts, which I then covered with
leaf litter, so as to not to not ruin the scene in the
photograph. Over two months, each evening I would
get into position in the hide with my camera and
flashguns ready for the badgers. Unfortunately, a
local rabbit discovered my operation and every night
helped itself to my peanuts, eventually reaching the
point where he would eat out of my hand. The rabbit
was not a tidy eater, he messed up what I had hoped
to be the perfect scene, as he rummaged through and
stole the nuts from under the leaves. On reflection I
see the funny side, but when I was sitting in the hide
each night watching the rabbit spoil my chance of
photographing badgers, I was far from amused.

Over the next two months, I returned at regular
intervals between nine in the evening and two-thirty
in the morning. I built up a portfolio of pictures of the
barn owl family, recording their breeding behaviour,
hatching and their first flight into the outside world.
It can never be overemphasised that extreme care
must be taken when photographing the natural world.
Environmental changes will only be accepted when
they are carried out gradually, with close attention to
the needs of the wildlife concerned.

I have experienced some magical moments with
nature, some frightening, others quite extraordinary.
My thoughts always return to a curlew that I was
photographing on a friend, George Wall's farm in
Weardale. Working on the fells with his livestock, he
was always aware of the many breeding species on
his farm. At that time I was compiling an audio-visual
programme on wildlife in the north east and at the
top of my wants list were pictures of breeding pairs
of curlews.

"No problem, I already have a hide up at a nest that
you are welcome to use" said George.

This saved precious time preparing a hide. Equipped
with a hide seat, tripod, camera equipment and a
flask, George 'installed' me into the hide for a six-hour
session.

The weather was cold, a typical May day on the fell
top. I had only been in the hide for fifteen
minutes, when the curlew came straight back
to her nest. Standing over her clutch of four

Over freindly rabbit

Atlantic grey seal bull